Father Raniero Cantalamessa O.F.M. Cap.

IN LOVE WITH CHRIST

Father Raniero Cantalamessa O.F.M. Cap.

IN LOVE WITH CHRIST
THE SECRET OF SAINT FRANCIS OF ASSISI

Rome 2014

ISBN-13: 978-0692229798
ISBN-10: 0692229795

PRESENTATION

The wave of enthusiasm and joy provoked by the new Pope's choice of the name "Francis" convinced me of the fittingness of dedicating to Saint Francis of Assisi the meditations given to the Pontifical household during Advent 2013.

The purpose is not celebratory but ecclesial and spiritual. It is to try to see what the life lived by this saint at the beginning of the 13th century still has to say to the Church of today, above all on the topic, so dear to the new Pope, of a simple and radical return to the Gospel. In his book "True and False Reform in the Church," the theologian Yves Congar sees the saint of Assisi as the clearest example of reform of the Church by way of holiness rather than criticism.

Although they were originally presented to a special audience that included the Pope, cardinals, bishops, prelates of the Roman curia and superiors general of religious orders, the reflections were developed with the whole Church in mind and, I think, are quite accessible to everyone. St. Francis is a universal man. During his life he preached to everyone, the learned and the ignorant, even to the birds and a wolf, according to Franciscan legend. One cannot speak of St. Francis except in a "Franciscan" way, hat is in a simple, direct and – possibly – even in a poetic way.

The blunt question that Brother Masseo asked St. Francis one day is well-known: "Why does everyone come to you? Why does the whole world run after you?" There is even more reason to pose the question today because the world that goes after the saint is no longer, as it was at that time, the little world of central Italy, but is, literally, the whole world, including many non-believers and members of other religions. The answer

that the Poverello gave to Brother Masseo –
"Because the eyes of God have not found a
more vile sinner on earth than me" – today
appears to us subjectively sincere but
objectively not true. The world, in reality, goes
after Francis of Assisi not because he was a
great sinner but because it sees the values that
everyone secretly aspires to realized in him:
peace, freedom, joy, universal brotherhood
and harmony with the whole creation.

In presenting these reflections to a wider
audience my intention is to show that there is
still another reason – the most important one
and the root of all other reasons – why people
go after Francis of Assisi. "After my death", the
philosopher Kierkegaard writes in his Journal,
"they will not find among my papers the
explication of what in reality has filled my life;
they will not find that word which tells
everything about me". We cannot say the same
of St. Francis. The explication of what filled his
life, the word which tells everything about him
- the "secret" of St. Francis - does exist: its
name is Jesus Christ! He reminds the world of

the humble and crucified Redeemer of whom he was a kind of living "icon". St. Francis of Assisi has been in an exemplary and unique way, what St. Paul says every Christian should be: "the good perfume of Christ in the world".

I

SAINT FRANCIS OF ASSISI AND THE RETURN TO THE GOSPEL

The aim of this first meditation is to highlight the nature of Francis' return to the Gospel. In his study on the "True and False Reform of the Church," the theologian Yves Congar sees in Francis the clearest example of the reform of the Church by way of holiness[1]. We wish to understand in what his reform by way of holiness consists and what his example implies in every age of the Church, including our own.

---

[1] Y. Congar, True and False Reform of the Church, Liturgical Press, 2010, part II, chap 1.

1. Francis' Conversion

To understand something of Francis' adventure it is necessary to begin with his conversion. Sources record different descriptions of this event, with notable variations between them. Fortunately we have an absolutely reliable source, which dispenses us from selecting among the different versions. We have the testimony of Francis himself in his Testament, his own *ipsissima vox*, as is said of Christ's words reliably reported in the Gospel. It says:

> "The Lord gave me, Brother Francis, thus to begin doing penance: for when I was in sin, it seemed too bitter for me to see lepers. And the Lord Himself led me among them and I showed mercy to them. And when I left them, what had seemed bitter to me was turned into sweetness of soul and body. And afterwards I delayed a little and left the world".[2]

---

[2] St. Francis of Assisi, Early Documents, I, New City Press, New York, London, Manila, 1999, p. 124 (hereafter quoted as ED + volume).

Historians rightly base themselves on this text, but there is one insurmountable limitation as far as they are concerned. Historians, even those with the best intentions and the highest respect for the unique qualities of Francis' life, such as Raoul Manselli among the Italians, fail to understand the ultimate reason for his radical change. They stop – and rightly so in accordance with their method – at the threshold, speaking of a "secret of Francis," destined to remain such forever.[3]

What can be proved historically, say the historians, is Francis' decision to change his social status. From belonging to the well-to-do class, which in the city counted as nobility and wealth, he chose to place himself at the opposite extreme, sharing the life of the lowliest ones, of those who did not count at all, the so-called "minors," afflicted by all sorts of poverty.

---

[3] R. Manselli, San Francesco d'Assisi, Editio Maior, Edizioni San Paolo 2002, pp. 114 s.

Historians rightly insist on the fact that in the beginning Francis did not choose poverty, and even less so pauperism; he chose the poor! The change was motivated more by the commandment: "Love they neighbor as thyself," than by the counsel: "If you wish to be perfect, go, sell all that you have and give it to the poor, then come and follow me." It was compassion for poor people, more than the search for his own perfection that moved him, charity more than poverty.

All this is true, but it still does not touch the core of the problem. It is the effect of the change, not its cause. The true choice is much more radical: it was not about choosing between wealth and poverty, or between the rich and the poor, between belonging to one class rather than another, but of choosing between himself and God, between saving his life or losing it for the Gospel.

There have been some (for instance, in times closer to us, Simone Weil) who came to Christ out of love for the poor and there have been others who came to the poor out of love for Christ. Francis belongs to the latter. The profound motive for his conversion was not of a social nature, but evangelical. Jesus had formulated the law once and for all in one of the most solemn and certainly most authentic phrases of the Gospel:

"If anyone wishes to come after Me, he must deny himself, take up his cross and follow Me. For whoever wishes to save his life will lose it; but whoever loses his life for My sake will find it". (*Matthew* 16: 24-25).

By kissing the leper, Francis denied himself in what was most "bitter" and repugnant to his nature. He did violence to himself. This fact did not escape his first biographer, who describes the episode thus:

"He met a leper one day. Made stronger than himself, he came up and kissed him. He then began to consider himself less and less, until by the mercy of the Redeemer, he came to complete victory over himself".[4]

---

[4] Celano, *Vita Prima*, VII, 17 (ED, I, p. 195).

Francis did not go to the lepers spontaneously, by his own will, but moved by human and religious compassion. "The Lord," he writes, "led me among them." It is on this small detail that historians are unable to give a judgment, but it is, in fact, at the origin of everything. Jesus had prepared Francis' heart so that his freedom would respond at the right moment to grace. Various incidents prepared him for it: the dream of Spoleto and the question whether he preferred to serve the servant or the master, his sickness, his imprisonment at Perugia and that strange anxiety that no longer allowed him to find joy in amusements and made him search for solitary places.

Without thinking that it was Jesus in person in the guise of a leper (as they later sought to do, thinking back to the similar case in the life of Saint Martin of Tours)[5], at that moment, for all intents and purposes, the leper represented Jesus for Francis. Francis' conversion is of the

---

[5] Celano, *Vita Secunda*, V,9 (ED, II, p. 249).

same nature as that of Paul. At a certain point, what for Paul had been a "gain" before changed into a "loss," "for the sake of Christ" (*Philippians* 3:5 ff.); for Francis, what had been bitter became sweetness, again "for the sake of Christ." After this moment, both can say: "It is no longer I who live, Christ lives in me."

All this obliges us to correct a certain image of Francis made popular by the subsequent literature and taken up by Dante in the Divine Comedy[6]. The famous metaphor of Francis' betrothal to Lady Poverty, which has left deep traces in Franciscan art and poetry, could lead us astray. You do not fall in love with a virtue, not even poverty; you fall in love with a person. Francis' nuptials were, as those of other mystics, a marriage with Christ.

---

[6] *Paradiso*, XI, vv. 58-74.

To companions who, seeing him one evening strangely absent and luminous, asked him if he intended to take a wife, the young Francis answered: "I will take the most noble and beautiful bride you have ever seen." This answer is usually interpreted wrongly. From the context it seems clear that the bride is not poverty, but the hidden treasure and the precious pearl, namely, Christ. "The unstained bride of god," comments Celano who refers to the episode, "is the true religion that he embraced, and the hidden treasure the kingdom of heaven that he sought with great longing."[7]

Francis did not wed poverty or even the poor; he wed Christ, and it was for love of him that he wed Lady Poverty, "in a second marriage" as it were. It will always be so in Christian holiness. If the love of poverty and of the poor is not based on love of Christ, the poor will be "used" in one way or another and poverty will easily become an issue against the

---

[7] Celano, *Vita Prima*, III, 7 (ED, I, p. 188).

Church, or a display of greater perfection compared to others in the Church, as happened, unfortunately, even with some of the *Poverello's* followers. In either case, poverty becomes one of the worst forms of wealth, where one is rich in one's own righteousness.

2. Francis and the Reform of the Church

How was it that such an interior and personal event as the conversion of the young Francis launched a movement that changed the face of the Church of his time and has had such a powerful effect in history up until our own day?

We must look at the situation at the time. In Francis' time, more or less everyone acknowledged the need for reform of the Church. Tensions and deep lacerations scarred the body of the Church. On one side was the institutional Church – Pope, Bishops, the higher clergy – worn out by perennial conflicts and by their very close alliance with the empire. It was a Church seen as distant, involved in matters far beyond the interests of the people. Then there were the great Religious Orders, among them the Cistercians, often flourishing because of their culture and spirituality after the various reforms of the 11th century, but fatally identified with the great landowners, the feudal lords of the time, both close to and at the same time remote from the problems and tenor of life of the common people.

On the opposite side there was a society that was beginning to emigrate from the countryside to the city in search of greater freedom from the different forms of servitude. This part of society identified the Church with the dominant classes from which they felt the need to free themselves. Because of this they would gladly take sides with those who contradicted her and fought against her: heretics, radical movements and groups that preached poverty, while they sympathized with the lower clergy, who were often spiritually not at the level of the prelates but closer to the people.

There were, therefore, strong tensions that everyone sought to exploit to their advantage. The hierarchy sought to respond to these tensions by improving its organization and suppressing the abuses, both within itself (combating simony and the concubinage of priests), and without, in society. The hostile groups sought instead to bring the tensions to a head, radicalizing the conflict with the hierarchy and giving rise to movements that were more or less schismatic. All of them used the ideal of evangelical poverty and simplicity against the Church, turning it into a polemical weapon, more than a spiritual ideal to be lived in humility, going so far as to question the ordained ministry of the Church, the priesthood and the papacy.

We are accustomed to seeing Francis as the man sent by providence who picks up these popular calls for renewal, defuses the voltage of controversy and brings them back into the Church, implementing them in profound communion and in submission to her. In this view, Francis is a sort of mediator between the rebellious heretics and the institutional Church. This is how his mission is presented in a well-known manual of Church history:

"Given that the wealth and power of the Church was often seen as a source of grave evils, and provided the heretics of the time with arguments for the main accusations against her, in some pious souls the noble desire was awakened to revive the poor life of Christ and of the primitive Church, and thus be able to influence the people more effectively by word and example."[8]

Among these souls, we naturally put Francis of Assisi in first place, together with Saint Dominic. The Protestant historian Paul Sabatier, for all his well-deserved place of honour in the field of Franciscan studies, has practically canonized among historians, - and

---

[8] K. Bihlmeyer – H. Tuchle, Storia della Chiesa, II, Brescia 2009. p. 239.

not only among the lay and Protestant ones - the thesis according to which Cardinal Ugolino (the future Gregory IX) intended to seize Francis for the Curia, domesticating the critical and revolutionary thrust of his movement.[9] In practice this was an attempt to turn Francis into a precursor of Luther, in other words, a reformer by way of criticism, rather than by holiness.

I do not know if this intention can be attributed to any of Francis' great protectors and friends. It seems difficult to attribute it to Cardinal Ugolino, much less to Innocent III, who is known for his reforming action and the support he gave to various new forms of spiritual life that arose in his time, including in fact the Friars Minor, the Dominicans and the Milanese Humiliati, In any case, one thing is absolutely certain: such an intention never crossed Francis' mind. He never thought of himself as called to reform the Church.

---

[9] Cf. P. Sabatier, Life of St. Francis of Assisi, New York, 1927.

One must be careful not to draw the wrong conclusions from the famous words of the Crucifix of San Damiano, "Francis, go and repair my Church, which as you see, is in ruins."[10] The sources themselves assure us that he understood those words in the rather modest sense of repairing the little church of San Damiano materially.

It was his disciples and biographers who interpreted those words – and rightly so, it must be said – as referring to the institutional Church, not just to the church building. He always kept to his literal interpretation and in fact continued to repair other small ruined churches on the outskirts of Assisi.

Even the dream of Innocent III, in which he is said to have seen the *Poverello* supporting the collapsing Church of the Lateran on his shoulders, does not tell us anything more. Supposing that the event is historical (a similar event is actually related about Saint

---

[10] Celano, *Vita Secunda*, VI,10 (ED, II, p. 249).

Dominic), the dream was the Pope's, not Francis'! He never saw himself as we see him today in Giotto's frescoes. This is what it means to be a reformer by way of holiness: being so without knowing it!

3. Francis and the Return to the Gospel

If he did not wish to be a reformer, what then did Francis want to be and do? Here too we are fortunate enough to have the Saint's direct testimony in his Testament:

> "And after the Lord gave me some brothers, no one showed me what I had to do; but the Most High Himself revealed to me that I should live according to the pattern of the Holy Gospel. And I had this written down simply and in a few words and the Lord Pope confirmed it for me."[11]

He alludes to the moment when, during Mass, he heard the passage of the Gospel

---

[11] The Testament, 14.15 (ED, I, p. 125).

where Jesus sends his disciples: "He sent them out to preach the Kingdom of God and to heal the sick. And he said to them, 'Take nothing for your journey, no staff, no bag, nor bread, nor money; and do not have two tunics" (*Luke* 9:2-3).[12] It was a dazzling revelation, the kind that gives direction to the whole of life. From that day onwards his mission was clear: a simple and radical return to the real Gospel lived and preached by Jesus; to restore in the world the way and style of life of Jesus and of the Apostles described in the Gospels. Writing the Rule for his friars, he began thus: "The Rule and life of the friars is this, namely to observe the holy Gospel of our Lord Jesus Christ".

Francis did not build a theory on his discovery, or turn it into a program for the reform of the Church. He accomplished the reform in himself, thus tacitly pointing out to the Church the only way out of the crisis: to

---

[12] The Legend of the Three Companions, VIII (ED,II, p. 84)

come close to the Gospel again, to come close again to the people and, in particular, to the humble and the poor.

This return to the Gospel is reflected first of all in Francis' preaching. It is surprising, but everyone has noted it: the *Poverello* almost always speaks of "doing penance." Celano tells us that "he then began to preach penance to all with such a fervent spirit and joyful attitude. He inspired his listeners with words that were simple and a heart that was heroic.[13] Wherever he went, Francis preached, recommended and begged his hearers to do penance.

What did Francis mean by these words, which were so close to his heart? On this matter we have fallen into error (at least I did, for a long time). We reduced Francis' message to mere moral exhortation, to a beating of the breast, scourging and mortifying oneself to atone for sin, when in fact it is as new and as

---

[13] Celano, *Vita Prima*, X (ED, I, p. 202).

vast in its scope as the Gospel of Christ itself. Francis did not exhort people to do "penances," but to do "penance" (in the singular!) which, as we shall see, is something else altogether.

With the exception of the few cases that we know of, the *Poverello* wrote in Latin. And what do we find in the Latin text of his Testament where he writes: "The Lord gave me, Brother Francis, to begin thus to do penance"? We find the expression *"poenitentiam agere."* We know that he loved to express himself in the very words of Jesus. And that word – to do penance – is the word with which Jesus began to preach and that he repeated in every city and village where he went:

> "After John was arrested, Jesus came into Galilee, preaching the Gospel of God, and saying, 'The time is fulfilled, and the kingdom of God is at hand; repent, and believe in the Gospel" (*Mark* 1:15).

The word that today is translated as "be

converted" or "repent," in the Vulgate text used by the *Poverello* sounded as "*poenitemini*" and in Acts 2:37 even more literally "*poenitentiam agite*," do penance. Francis did nothing other than re-launch the great appeal to conversion with which Jesus' preaching opens in the Gospel, and that of the Apostles on the day of Pentecost. He did not need to explain what he meant by conversion: his whole life showed it.

Francis did in his day what was intended at the time of Vatican Council II by the motto: "pull down the bastions": put an end to the isolation of the Church and bring her back into contact with the people. One of the factors that obscured the Gospel was the transformation of authority understood as service, into authority understood as power, which produced endless conflicts within and outside the Church. Francis, for his part, resolved the problem evangelically. In his Order – and this was totally new - the Superiors would be called ministers, that is, servants, and all the others, friars, meaning brothers.

Another wall of separation between the Church and the people was the monopoly of knowledge and culture held, in practice, by the clergy and monks. Francis knew this, which is why he took the drastic position on this point which we know well. He had no problem with knowledge as such, but with knowledge as power; the kind that places a man who could read over one who could not, and allowed him to look down on his brother and proudly order him to: "Bring me the Breviary!" During the famous chapter of mats some of his brothers tried to persuade him to adopt the attitude of the learned Orders of the time. He answered them with words of fire that left the brothers overcome with fear:

"My brothers! My brothers! God has called me by the way of simplicity and showed me the way of simplicity. I do not want you to mention to me any Rule, whether of Saint Augustine, or of Saint Bernard, or of Saint Benedict. And the Lord told me what He wanted: He wanted me to be a new fool in the world. God did not wish to lead us by any other than this knowledge, but God will confound you by your knowledge and wisdom".[14]

He always had the same consistent attitude. For himself and his brothers he wanted the most rigid poverty, but he exhorts them in the Rule "not to despise or judge those whom they see dressed in soft and fine clothes and enjoying the choicest food and drink, but rather let everyone judge and despise himself".[15] He chose to be an illiterate, but did not condemn knowledge. Once he was assured that knowledge would not extinguish "the spirit of holy prayer and devotion," he himself allowed Brother Anthony (the future St. Anthony of Padua) to devote himself to teaching theology[16], and Saint Bonaventure did not believe he was betraying the spirit of the founder by opening the Order to studies in the great universities.

---

[14] *Legenda Perusina*, 114 (ED, II, 132 s.).

[15] *Regula Bullata*, chap. II (ED, I, 101).

[16] A Letter to Brother Anthony of Padua (ED,I, p. 107).

Yves Congar sees in this one of the essential conditions of "true reform" in the Church, namely, it remains exactly that, and does not turn into schism: in other words, the capacity not to make an absolute of one's own insight, but to remain in communion with the whole which is the Church.[17] This is the conviction, as Pope Francis says in his recent Apostolic Exhortation *Evangelii gaudium*, that "the whole is greater than the part."

4. How to Imitate Francis

What does Francis' experience say to us today? What can we – all of us, right now – imitate in his life? Be it those whom God calls to reform the Church by the way of holiness, or those who feel called to renew her by way of criticism, or again those he himself calls to reform her through the office they hold? The same thing with which Francis' spiritual adventure began: his conversion from ego to

---

[17] Cfr. Congar, op. cit, pp. 177 ss).

God, his denial of self. This is how true reformers are born, those who really change something in the Church: they are people who are dead to themselves. Or rather, they are those who seriously decide to die to themselves, because it is an enterprise that lasts a lifetime and beyond, if, as Saint Teresa of Avila jokingly said, our self-love dies 20 minutes after we do.

Silvanus of Mount Athos, a holy Orthodox monk, said: "To be truly free, one must begin to bind oneself." Men such as these are free with the freedom of the Spirit; nothing stops them and nothing frightens them anymore. They become reformers by way of holiness, and not only by way of office.

But what does Jesus mean by proposing that one deny oneself? Is such a proposal still valid in a world that speaks only of self-realization, self-affirmation? Denial is never an end in itself, or an ideal in itself. The most important thing is the positive part: *If anyone wants to be a follower of mine*; it is to follow

Christ, to possess Christ. To say no to oneself is the means; to say yes to Christ is the end. Paul represents it as a sort of law of the spirit: "If with the help of the Spirit you put to death the deeds of the body you will live" (*Romans* 8:13). This, as we see, is a dying in order to live; the very opposite of the philosophical view of human life as "a living to die" (Heidegger).

It is all about knowing the foundation on which we want to build our lives: on our "ego" or "on Christ"? In Paul's language, do we want to live "for ourselves" or "for the Lord"? (cf. 2 *Corinthians* 5:15; *Romans* 14:7-8). To live "for ourselves" means to live for our own comfort, our own glory, our own advancement; to live "for the Lord" means that in our intentions we always put Christ's glory first, and the interests of the Kingdom and of the Church. Every "no" said to oneself out of love, small or big as it may be, is a yes said to Christ.

We must not delude ourselves. It is not a matter of knowing everything about Christian denial, about how beautiful and necessary it is; the point is we must do something about it, and put it into practice. A great ancient spiritual teacher said: "In a short time one may cut off ten of one's own desires, and I will tell you how.

Let us suppose that someone is walking a short distance; he sees something and the thought says to him, "Look over there." He replies to the thought, "I will not look," and he cuts off his desire and does not look. Or he meets some others who are talking idly among themselves and the thought says to him, "You say a word also," but he cuts off his desire and does not speak."[18]

This ancient Father gives examples drawn from the monastic life. But they can be easily updated and adapted to the life of everyone, clergy and laity. Let us say you meet, perhaps not a leper like Francis, but a poor man who you know very well will ask you for something;

---

[18] Dorotheus of Gaza, Spiritual Works, I, 20 (SCh 92, p. 177).

your old nature pushes you to cross to the other side of the street, but, instead, you do violence to yourself and go to meet him, perhaps giving him only a greeting or a smile, if you cannot do more. Or you are given an opportunity to profit from something illegally: say no and you have denied yourself. You are contradicted in one of your ideas; wounded in your pride, you want to fight back strongly; be silent and wait: you have broken your ego. You believe you have been wronged, treated unjustly and not given the job you deserve: you want everyone to know about it, to shut yourself off in a silent rebuke. Say no, break the silence, smile and reopen the dialogue. You have denied yourself and saved charity. And so on.

One sign of progress in the struggle against our ego is the capacity, or at least the effort, to rejoice at the good done or the promotion received by another, as if it were our own.

"Blessed is that servant," writes Francis in one of his Admonitions, "who no more exalts himself over the good the Lord says or does through him than over what He says or does through another".[19]

A difficult goal (I am far from having reached it myself), but Francis' experience has shown us what can come from the denial of self in response to grace. The prize is the joy of being able to say with Paul and with Francis: "It is no longer I who live, but Christ lives in me." (*Gal* 2:20) And it will mean the beginnings of joy and peace, already here on earth. With his "perfect joy", Francis is a living witness to "the joy of the Gospel", the *Evangelii gaudium*.

---

[19] Admonitions XVII (ED, I, p. 134).

II

HUMILITY AS TRUTH AND SERVICE IN FRANCIS OF ASSISI

1. Objective and Subjective Humility

Let us listen to an episode narrated in the charming style of the Fioretti, the Little Flowers of St. Francis:

"One day, as Saint Francis was returning from the woods, where he had been praying. Brother Masseo, wishing to test the humility of the saint, went up to him and half jokingly said: "Why after you? Why after you?" Saint Francis replied:

"What do you mean?" Brother Masseo answered: "I mean, why does the whole world come after you; and everyone seems to desire to see you and hear you? You aren't a handsome man in body, you aren't someone of great learning, you're not noble, so why does the whole world run after you?" Hearing this, Saint Francis was overjoyed in spirit [...] he turned to Brother Masseo and said: "Do you want to know why they come after me? ... I have this from the eyes of the Most High God, which gaze in every place on the good and the guilty: because those most holy eyes have not seen among sinners anyone more vile, nor more incompetent, nor a greater sinner than me"[1]

The question is more justified today than it was in Br. Masseo's day. At that time, the "world" that chased after Francis was the small world of Umbria and central Italy; today it is literally the whole world, often even the world of unbelievers or those of other religions. The

---

[1] The Little Flowers of St. Francis, chap. X, 8 (ED, III, 583).

Poverello's answer was sincere but not true. In reality the whole world is fascinated by the personality of St. Francis not because it is convinced that he was the greatest sinner of all, but because it sees values fulfilled in him to which every human being aspires: freedom, joy, peace with one self and the whole of creation, universal brotherhood.

We are now going to speak of a quality of St. Francis which the world doesn't aspire to at all, but which on contrary is the root from which all his other qualities spring: his humility. According to Dante Alighieri, who dedicated to St. Francis one of the most inspired poems of his *Divine Comedy*, all the glory of Francis depends on his having made himself "pusillo" little,"[2] in other words, on his humility.

But what did Saint Francis' proverbial humility consist of? In all the languages through which the bible has passed on its

---

[2] Paradise, XI, 111.

journey to us, namely Hebrew, Greek, Latin and English, the word "humility" has two fundamental meanings: one *is objective*, and indicates lowliness, littleness or poverty, and one *subjective*, indicating the sense and recognition a person has of his or her own littleness. The latter is what we understand by the virtue of humility.

When Mary says in the *Magnificat*: "He has regarded the humility (*tapeinosis*) of his handmaid," she means humility in the objective sense, not the subjective! Because of this, in many languages the term is very appropriately translated as "littleness", not as humility. Moreover, how can one imagine that Mary exalts her humility and attributes God's choice to it without by that very fact destroying her humility? And yet at times it has been carelessly written that Mary recognizes in herself no other virtue than humility, as though this honoured humilty, rather than doing it great harm.

The virtue of humility has an altogether

special status: it is possessed by those who think they do not have it, and those who think they have it do not possess it. Jesus alone can declare himself "lowly of heart" and truly be so; this, we shall see, is the unique and unrepeatable characteristic of the humility of the Man-God. Did Mary therefore not have the *virtue* of humility? She certainly did, and in the highest degree, but only God knew this, she did not. In fact, the incomparable quality of true humility consists precisely in the fact that its perfume is perceived only by God, not by the one who emanates it. Saint Bernard wrote: "The truly humble man is anxious not to be acclaimed for his humility, but to be reputed as vile."[3] Francis' humility, as the dialogue with Brother Masseo has shown us, is precisely of this kind.

---

[3] St. Bernard, Sermons on the Canticle, XVI,10 (PL 183, 853).

2. Humility as Truth

Two sources shed light on Francis' humility; one is theological, the other Christological in nature. Let us reflect on the first. We find in the Bible acts of humility that do not come from man, from the consideration of his misery or his own sin, but which have God and God's holiness as their sole origin. Such is Isaiah's exclamation, "I am a man of unclean lips," when he was faced in the Temple with the sudden manifestation of God's glory and holiness (*Isaiah* 6:5 f). Such also is Peter's cry to Jesus after the miraculous catch: "Depart from me, for I am a sinful man!" (*Luke* 5:8).

Here we are faced with the essence of humility, that of the creature who becomes conscious of himself in the presence of God. As long as a person measures himself by his own standards, by other people or by society, he will never have a correct idea of what he is; the yardstick is missing. "What an infinite accent falls upon the self", wrote Kierkegaard, "by having God as a measure".[4] Francis possessed this humility in an outstanding degree. A saying that he often repeated was: "What a person is before God, that he is and no more."[5]

The *Little Flowers* describe how one night Brother Leo wanted to spy on Francis from a distance to see what he did during his night prayer in the forest of La Verna, and from a distance he heard him murmuring some words for a long time. Next day the Saint called him and, after gently reprimanding him for having disobeyed his order, revealed to him the content of his prayer:

> "Little Brother Lamb of Jesus Christ, in those things which you saw and heard when I said those words, two lights were shown to my soul: one of the knowledge and understanding of the Creator, and the

---

[4] S. Kierkegaard, The Sickness unto Death, II, 1, 1.

[5] St. Francis, Admonitions, XIX (ED, I, p. 135); see also St. Bonaventure, The Mayor Legend, VI, 1 (ED, II, p. 569).

other of the knowledge of myself. When I said, 'Who are You, my dearest God?', I was then in a light of contemplation in which I saw the depths of the infinite goodness and wisdom and power of God. And when I said, 'What am I?' I was in a light of contemplation in which I saw the grievous depths of my vileness and misery"[6]

This was the gift Saint Augustine had asked of God and which he considered the height of all wisdom: "*Noverim me, noverim te*. Let me know myself and let me know You; let me know myself in order to humble myself, and let me know You in order to love You."[7]

The episode of Brother Leo is certainly embellished, as is always the case in *The Little Flowers*, but the content corresponds perfectly with the idea that Francis had of himself and of God. Proof of this is found at the beginning

---

[6] The Considerations on the Holy Stigmata, III (in St. Francis of Assisi, Omnibus of Sources, Chicago 1972, p. 1446).

[7] St. Augustine, *Soliloqui*, I,1,3; II,1,1 (PL 32, 870. 885).

of the Canticle of the Creatures, in the infinite distance that he puts between God, "Most High, Omnipotent, Good Lord" and the miserable mortal who is not even worthy of pronouncing his name:

> Most High, all-powerful, good Lord,
> Yours are the praise, the glory, and the honor, and all blessing,
> To you alone, Most High, do they belong,
> And no human is worthy to mention Your name[8].

In this light, what I have called theological humility appears to us essentially as truth. "I asked myself one day," wrote Saint Teresa of Avila, "why the Lord loves humility so much and suddenly there came to my mind, without any reflection on my part, that it must be because he is total Truth, and humility is truth."[9]

It is a light that does not humiliate but, on

---

[8] The Canticle of Creatures (ED, I, p. 113).

[9] St. Theresa of Avila, Interior Castle, VI, chap.10.

the contrary, gives immense joy and exalts. To be humble in fact does not mean to be unhappy with oneself or to recognize one's own misery, or even one's littleness. It is to look at God before oneself and to plumb the depths of the gulf that separates the finite from the infinite. The more one realizes this, the more one becomes humble. Then one even begins to enjoy one's own nothingness, because, thanks to it, a face can be presented to God whose littleness and misery has fascinated the heart of the Trinity from all eternity.

Angela of Foligno, a great disciple of the *Poverello*, whom Pope Francis recently proclaimed a Saint, exclaimed on her deathbed: "O unknown nothingness, O unknown nothingness. Truly a soul cannot have a better awareness in this world than to perceive its own nothingness and to reside there as in a cell."[10] There is a secret in this

---

[10] Angela of Foligno, Complete Works, Paulist Press, New York 1993, p. 315 s.

counsel, a truth that is tested by experiencing it. One then discovers that this cell really exists and that one can truly enter it every time one wishes. It consists in the quiet and tranquil sense of being nothing before God, but a "nothing" that is loved by Him!

When one is inside this light-filled cell, one no longer sees one's neighbor's defects, or they are seen in a different light. One understands that it is possible, with grace and practice, to accomplish what the Apostle says, which at first glance seems excessive, namely, to "consider all others better than oneself" (cf. *Philippians* 2:3). At least one understands how this was possible for the saints.

To be locked inside that prison is, therefore, altogether different from being locked in oneself; Quite the contrary, it means opening oneself to others, to the being, the objectivity of things. It is the opposite of what the enemies of Christian humility have always thought. It is to close oneself to egoism, not in egoism. It is the victory over one of the evils that even modern psychology judges harmful to the human person: narcissism. Into that cell, moreover, the enemy cannot penetrate. One day Anthony the Great had a vision; he saw in an instant all the infinite snares of the enemy spread out over the earth and, moaning, he said: "Who will be able to avoid all these snares?" And he heard a voice answer him: "Humility!"[11] "Nothing", writes the author of the Imitation of Christ, "will succeed in puffing up one who is firmly rooted in God."[12]

3. Humility in the Service of Love

We have talked about humility as the true state of the creature before God. Paradoxically, however, what most fills Francis' soul with wonder is not God's greatness but his humility. In the *Praises of God Most High*,

---

[11] *Apophtegmata Patrum*, Antonius 7 (PG 65, 77).

[12] Imitation of Christ, II, 10.

handwritten by him and preserved in Assisi, among God's perfections – "You are Holy, You are Strong. You are Triune and One. You are Love, Charity. You are Wisdom ...", at a certain point Francis inserts one that is unheard-of: "You are humility!" It is not a title put there by mistake. Francis grasped a most profound truth about God which should also fill us with wonder.

God is humility because He is love. In the face of human creatures, God finds himself without any coercive or defensive capacity. If human beings choose to reject his love, as they have done, He cannot intervene with authority to impose Himself on them. He can do nothing other than respect the free human choice. One can reject Him, eliminate Him: He will not defend Himself, He will let them do it. Or better, his way of defending himself and of defending men against their very annihilation, will be that of loving again and always, eternally. By its nature love creates dependence and dependence creates humility. So it is also, mysteriously, in God.

Love therefore provides the key to understand God's humility: it doesn't take much skill to show off, but to stand aside, to leave no trace of self, requires great strength. God is this unlimited power of self-concealment, and as such He reveals himself in the Incarnation. One has the visible manifestation of God's humility by contemplating Christ who kneels before his disciples to wash their feet – and we can presume they were dirty feet. Even more is God's humility revealed when, reduced to the utmost impotence on the cross, He continues to love, without ever condemning.

Francis grasped this very close connection between God's humility and the Incarnation. Here are some of his impassioned words:

> "Behold, each day He humbles Himself as when He came from the royal throne into the Virgin's womb; each day He Himself comes to us, appearing humbly; each day He comes down from the bosom of the Father upon the altar in the hands of a

priest."[13]

"O sublime humility! O humble sublimity! The Lord of the universe, God and Son of God, so humbles Himself that for our salvation He hides Himself under an ordinary piece of bread. Brothers, look at the humility of God and pour out your hearts before Him!"[14]

Thus we have discovered the second reason for Francis' humility: the example of Christ. It is the same reason that Paul suggested to the Philippians when he recommended that they have the same sentiments as Christ Jesus who "*humbled* himself and became obedient unto death" (*Philippians* 2:5.8). Before Paul, it was Jesus himself who invited the disciples to imitate his humility: "Learn from me, for I am gentle and humble in heart!" (*Matthew* 11:29).

---

[13] Admonitions, I, (ED, I, p. 129).

[14] Letter to the Entire Order (ED, I, p. 118).

We may wonder exactly how Jesus is asking us to imitate his humility. In what way was Jesus humble? Nowhere in the Gospels do we find even the slightest admission of guilt on Jesus' lips, either in his conversations with people, or when he converses with his Father. This, by the way, is one of the most hidden but also most convincing proofs of Christ's divinity and of the absolute uniqueness of his conscience. In no saint, in no great man in history and in no religious founder does one find such an awareness of innocence.

All acknowledge, more or less, that they have made mistakes or need to be forgiven for something, at least by God. Gandhi, for instance, had a very acute awareness of having taken wrong positions on occasion; even he had his regrets. Jesus never did. He could say to his adversaries: "Which of you convicts me of sin?" (*John* 8:46). Jesus proclaims he is "Teacher and Lord" (cf. *John* 13:13), that he is more than Abraham, more than Moses, more than Jonah, greater than Solomon. Where, then, is Jesus' humility, so that he can say:

"learn from me who am humble?"

Here we discover something important. Humility does not consist mainly in *being small* -- one can be small without being humble; nor does it consist principally in *feeling small*, because one can feel small when one actually is small, and that would be an objective statement, but not yet humility. To say nothing of the fact that feeling small and insignificant could stem from an inferiority complex and lead one to withdraw into oneself and to despair, rather than to humility. Therefore humility per se, in the most perfect degree, lies not in being small, nor in feeling small or proclaiming oneself small. It lies in *making* oneself small, not out of some necessity or personal advantage, but out of love, in order to "raise up" others.

Thus was Jesus' humility; He made himself so small, in fact, that he "emptied" himself for us. Jesus' humility is the humility that descends from God and that has its supreme model in God, not in man. In the position in which He finds himself, God cannot "elevate himself"; nothing exists above Him. If God comes out of Himself and does something outside the Trinity, this can only be a lowering of himself and making himself small; in other words, He can only be humility, or as some Greek Fathers said, *synkatabasis*, that is, condescendence.

Saint Francis made "Sister Water" the symbol of humility, describing it as "useful, humble, precious and chaste." Water, in fact, never "elevates" itself, never "ascends," but always "descends," until it has found the lowest point. Steam rises, and that is why it is the traditional symbol of pride and vanity; water descends and is, therefore, the symbol of humility.

Now we know what Jesus' word means: "Learn from me for I am humble." It is an invitation to make oneself small out of love, to wash the feet of our brothers and sisters, as he did. However, in Jesus we also see the seriousness of this choice. It is not in fact about descending and making oneself small every now and then, like a king who, in his generosity, every so often deigns to come down among the people and perhaps also to serve them in some way. Jesus makes himself "small," as "he made himself flesh," that is permanently, to the end. He chooses to belong to the *category* of the little ones and the humble.

This new face of humility is summarized in one word: service. One day – we read in the Gospel – the disciples discussed among themselves who was "the greatest". Then Jesus "sat down" (so as to give greater solemnity to the lesson he was about to impart), called the Twelve together and said to them: "If anyone wants to be first, he must be last of all and servant of all" (*Mark* 9:35). He who wishes to be "first" must be "last," that is, must descend, must lower himself. But then he immediately explains what he means by *last*: he must be the "servant" of all. The humility proclaimed by Jesus is, therefore, service. In Matthew's Gospel, this lesson of Jesus is confirmed with an example: "just as the Son of man came not to be served but to serve" (*Matthew* 20:28).

4. A Humble Church

Let us draw some practical considerations on the virtue of humility in all its manifestations, whether in relation to God or to people. We must not make the mistake of thinking we have attained humility just because the word of God has led us to discover our nothingness and has taught us that it must show itself in fraternal service. We see the extent to which we have attained humility when the initiative passes from us to others, namely when it is no longer we who recognize our defects and wrongs, but others do so; when we are not only able to tell ourselves the truth, but also gladly let others do so. Before acknowledging himself to Brother Masseo as the vilest of men, Francis had gladly and for a long time accepted being laughed at, held by friends, relatives and the whole town of Assisi to be ungrateful, proud, one who would never do anything good in life.

In other words, the point we are at in the struggle against pride is seen in the way we react, externally or internally, when we are contradicted, corrected, criticized or ignored. To claim to kill your pride by striking it yourself, without anyone intervening from outside, is like using your own arm to punish yourself: you will never do yourself any real harm. It is as if a doctor tried to remove a tumor from his own body on his own.

When I look for glory from a human being for something I say or do, it is almost certain that the person before me is looking for glory from me because of the way he listens or the way he responds. And so it is that everyone seeks his own glory and no one obtains it and if, by chance, he does obtain it, it is nothing but "vainglory," that is, empty glory, destined to go up in smoke at the moment of death. However, the effect is equally terrible; in fact Jesus attributed the inability to believe to the search for one's glory. He asked the Pharisees: "How can you believe, since you look for glory from one another, and do not seek the glory that comes from the one God?" (*John* 5:44).

When we find ourselves once again embroiled in thoughts and aspirations to human glory, we must throw into the mix, like a burning torch, the word that Jesus himself used and that he left us: "I do not seek my own glory!" (*John* 8:50). The struggle for humility lasts a lifetime and touches every aspect of life. Pride can feed on evil or on goodness; in fact, unlike what happens with every other vice, goodness, not evil, is the preferred culture for this terrible "virus." The philosopher Pascal wrote wittily:

> "Vanity is so anchored in the human heart that a soldier, a soldier's servant, a cook or a porter brags and wishes to have his admirers. Even philosophers wish for them. Those who write against it want to have the glory of having written well; and those who read it desire the glory of having read it. I who write these words perhaps have the

same desire, and perhaps too, those who will read them..."[15].

So that a man "will not get above himself," God often fixes him to the ground with a sort of anchor; He puts alongside him, as He did with Paul, a "messenger of Satan to harass him," "a thorn in the flesh" (2 *Corinthians* 12:7). We do not know exactly what this "thorn in the flesh" was for the Apostle, but we know well enough what it means for us! Everyone who wants to follow the Lord and serve the Church has one. We are talking about those humiliating situations which constantly called back, sometimes night and day, to face the harsh reality of what we are. It can be a defect, a sickness, a weakness, a manifestation of powerlessness, which the Lord leaves with us, despite all our pleas; a persistent and humiliating temptation, perhaps a temptation to pride; a person one is forced to live with and who, despite the integrity of both parties, has the power to expose our fragility and demolish

---

[15] B. Pascal, Pensees, n. 150, ed. Brunschwicg.

our presumption.

However, humility is not a private virtue. There is a kind of humility that must shine out in the Church as an institution and as people of God. If God is humility, the Church, too, must be humility; if Christ served, the Church must also serve, and serve out of love. For too long the Church as a whole has represented before the world the *truth* of Christ, but perhaps she has not represented sufficiently the *humility* of Christ. Yet humility, better than any arguments or discussions, disarms hostility and prejudice in her regard and the way is smoothed for the acceptance of the Gospel.

There is an episode in Manzoni's novel *The Betrothed* which contains a profound psychological and evangelical truth. The Capuchin brother Christopher, having finished his novitiate, decides to ask forgiveness publicly from the parents of a man whom he had killed in a duel before becoming a friar. The family lines up, as in a latter-day defeat of the Roman armies, so that the gesture will be as humiliating as possible for the friar and bring the greatest satisfaction to the family's pride. But when they see the young friar walk forward with his head bowed, kneeling before the brother of the man who was killed, and asking for forgiveness, their arrogance falls away, and they are the ones who feel embarrassed and apologize, so that in the end all crowd around the friar to commend themselves to his prayers.[16] These are the miracles of humility.

In the prophet Zephaniah God says: "But in you I shall leave surviving a humble and lowly people. They shall seek refuge in the name of the Lord" (*Zephaniah* 3:12). This word is still timely and perhaps the success of the evangelization to which the Church is committed will depend on it.

Now, before I finish, I need to remind myself of a saying that was dear to Saint

---

[16] A. Manzoni, The Betrothed, chap. IV.

Francis. He used to repeat: "The Emperor Charles, Roland, and Oliver, and all the paladins and valiant knights who were mighty in battle, pursuing unbelievers with great toil and fatigue even to death, had a glorious and memorable victory [...] And there are many who want to receive honor and praise by only relating what they did."[17] He used this example to say "the saints accomplished great things and we want only to receive glory and honor by recounting them."[18]

To avoid being reckoned as one of them, I have tried to put into practice the advice given by an ancient desert Father, Isaac of Nineveh, to one who was obliged because of his office to speak of spiritual things which he had not yet attained in his own life: "Speak, he said, as one who belongs to the category of disciples, and not with authority, after humbling your soul and making yourself smaller than any of your

---

[17] The Assisi Compilation, 103 [= *Legenda Perugina* 72] (ED II, 209).

[18] Admonitions, VI (ED, I, p. 131).

listeners."[19] In this spirit, Holy Father, Venerable Fathers, brothers and sisters, I have dared to speak to you of humility.

---

[19] Isaac of Nineve, Ascetic discourses, 4 (Città Nuova, Roma 1984, p.89).

III

St. FRANCIS, THE INCARNATION AND THE POOR

1. Greccio and the Institution of the Crib

We all know Francis' story at Greccio where, three years before his death, he initiated the Christmas tradition of the Crib, but it is good to recall it for the highest leaders in this circumstance. Well, Celano wrote:

> "There was a certain man in that area [Rieti] named John, who had a good reputation but an even better manner of life. Blessed Francis loved him with special

affection [...] Around fifteen days prior to the birthday of the Lord, Francis sent for him and said to him, "If you wish to celebrate the approaching feast of the Lord at Greccio, hurry and carefully prepare the things I tell you. For I wish to enact the memory of that babe who was born in Bethlehem, to see as much as is possible with my own bodily the discomfort of his infant needs, how he lay in the manger, and how with an ox and an ass standing by, he rested on hay." [...] The manger is prepared, hay is carried in, and the ox and ass are led to the spot. There,. simplicity is given a place of honour, poverty is exalted, humility is commended and out of Greccio a new Bethlehem is made. [...].The holy man of God is drwessed in a deacon's vestments, since he was a deacon, and with full voice he sings the holy gospel. And his voice, a powerful voice, a pleasant voice, a clear voice, a musical voice, invites all to the highest of gifts. Then he preaches to the people standing around him, and pours forth sweet honey about the birth of the poor king and the poor city of Bethlehem".[1]

---

[1] Celano, *Vita Prima*, 84-85 (ED,I, p-254 s.).

The importance of the episode lies not so much in the fact itself or in the spectacular consequences it has had in the Christian tradition; it lies in the novelty that it reveals in the Saint's understanding of the mystery of the Incarnation. The one-sided insistence, excessive and at times downright obsessive, on the ontological aspects of the Incarnation, (nature, person, hypostatic union, communication of properties) had often made one lose sight of the true nature of the Christian mystery, reducing it to a speculative mystery, to be formulated with ever more rigorous categories, but far beyond the capacity of the people.

Francis of Assisi helps us to integrate the ontological vision of the Incarnation with the more existential and religious vision. In fact, it is not only important to know _that God became man, it is important to know also what type of man he became_. Significant are the different and complementary ways in which John and Paul describe the event of the Incarnation. For John it consists in the fact that the Word who was God was made flesh (cf. *John* 1:1-14); for Paul it consists in the fact that "Christ, being of divine nature, took the form of a servant and he humbled himself and became obedient unto death" (cf. *Philippians* 2:5 ff.). For John, the Word, being God, became man; for Paul "Christ, though he was rich, became poor" (cf. 2 *Corinthians* 8:9).

Francis of Assisi has his place as a spiritual descendent of Saint Paul. More than on the ontological *reality* of the humanity of Christ (in which he believed firmly along with the whole Church), he insisted, to the point of becoming emotional, on the *humility and poverty* of his humanity. The sources say that two things had the power to move him to tears every time he heard them mentioned: "the humility of the Incarnation and the charity of the Passion."[2] "He could not recall without tears the great want surrounding the little poor Virgin on that day. One day when he was sitting down to dinner a brother mentioned

---

[2] Ib. 84 (ED, I, p. 254).

the poverty of the blessed Virgin, and reflected on the want of Christ her Son. No sooner had he heard this than he got up from the table, groaning with sobs of pain, and bathed in tears ate the rest of his bread on the naked ground."[3]

Thus, Francis restored "flesh and blood" to the mysteries of Christianity, which were often "disincarnate" and reduced to concepts and syllogisms in theological schools and books. A German scholar has seen in Francis the one who created the conditions for the birth of modern Renaissance art, in as much as it frees sacred persons and events from the stylized rigidity of the past and confers on them concreteness and life.[4]

[3] Celano, *Vita Secunda*, 151 (ED,II, p.375).

[4] H. Thode, Franz of Assisi und die Anfänge der Kunst des Renaissance in Italien, Berlin 1885.

2. Christmas and the Poor

The distinction between the *fact* of the Incarnation and the *manner* of it, between its ontological and its existential dimension, is of interest to us because it casts a singular light on the present-day problem of poverty and the attitude of Christians towards it. It helps to give a biblical and theological foundation to the preferential option for the poor, proclaimed by the Second Vatican Council. If, indeed, by the *fact* of the Incarnation, the Word has, in a certain sense, assumed every man, as certain Fathers of the Church said, because of the *way* in which the Incarnation happened, the Word assumed, under an altogether particular title, the poor, the humble, the suffering, to the point of identifying himself with them.

St. Francis was so conscious of this that one day he said to a companion who had ill-judged a poor man: "Whenever you see a poor person you ought to consider Him in whose name he comes, that is, Christ, who came to take on our

<u>poverty and weakness</u>. This man's poverty and weakness is a mirror for us in which we should see and consider lovingly the poverty and weakness of our Lord Jesus Christ, which He endured in His body for the salvation of the human race."[5]

In the poor there is certainly not the same kind of presence of Christ that there is in the Eucharist and in the other Sacraments, but it is a presence that is also true, "real." He "instituted" this sign, as he instituted the Eucharist. He who pronounced over the bread the words: "This is my Body," said these same words also referring to the poor. He said them when, speaking of what had been done or not done, for the hungry, the thirsty, for prisoners, the naked and the exiled, he solemnly declared: "You did it to me" and "You did not do it to me." This, in fact, is the same as saying: "I was that wounded person in need of some bread, that old man who was dying with cold on the sidewalk!" "The Council Fathers,"

---

[5] *Legenda Perusina*, 89 (ED, II, p. 221).

wrote Jean Guitton, a lay observer at Vatican II, "rediscovered the sacrament of poverty, the presence of Christ under the species of those who suffer."[6]

The poor person is also a "vicar of Christ," one who takes the place of Christ, a vicar in the passive, not the active sense. In other words, not in the sense that what the poor person does is as if Christ did it, but in the sense that what is done to the poor person is as if it were done to Christ. It is true, as Saint Leo the Great wrote, that after the Ascension, "all that was visible in our Lord Jesus Christ has passed into the sacramental signs of the Church,"[7] but it is equally true that, from the existential point of view it has also passed onto the poor and onto all those of whom he said: "you did it to me."

Let us draw the consequence that derives

---

[6] J. Guitton, quoted by R. Gil, Presence of the Poor in the Council, in "Proyeccion" 48, 1966, p. 30.

[7] St. Leo the Great, Discourse 2 on the Ascension, 2 (PL 54, 398).

from all this on the level of ecclesiology. At the Council, John XXIII coined the expression "the Church of the poor."[8] It has a meaning that perhaps goes beyond what we understand at first sight. The Church of the poor is not composed only of the poor of the Church! In a certain sense, all the poor of the world, whether they are baptized or not, belong to her. Their poverty and suffering is their baptism of blood. If Christians are those who have been "baptized into the death of Christ" (*Romans* 6:3), who in fact is more baptized than they are in the death of Christ?

How can they not be considered, in some way, as the Church of Christ, if Christ himself has declared them to be his body? They are "Christians," not because they declare themselves as belonging to Christ, but because Christ has declared them as belonging to himself: "You did it to me!" If there is one case to which the controversial expression "anonymous Christians" can be plausibly

---

[8] In AAS 54,1962, p.682.

applied, it is in fact this one of the poor.

Hence, the Church of Christ is immensely vaster than what the current statistics show. Not just in a manner of speaking, but truly, really. No religious founder identified himself with the poor as Jesus did. No one proclaimed: "All that you did to one of the least of these my brethren, you did it to me" (*Matthew* 25:40), where the "least brother" does not mean only a believer in Christ but as all admit, every person.

From this it follows that the Pope, the Vicar of Christ, is truly the "Father of the poor," the shepherd of this immense flock, and it is a joy and a stimulus for all Christian people to see how much this role has been taken to heart by the last Supreme Pontiffs and in an altogether particular way, by the shepherd who sits today on Peter's Chair. His is the most authoritative voice that is raised in their defense, the voice of those who do not have a voice. He certainly has not "forgotten the poor"!

We tend to put double glazing between us and the poor. The effect of double glazing, so much in use today in the building industry, is that it impedes the passage of cold, of heat, of noise, it dilutes everything, it deadens and muffles every sound. And in fact we see the poor moving, bustling about, crying out, on our television screens, on the pages of newspapers and missionary magazines, but their cries are a distant echo that never reaches our hearts. I say this to my own embarrassment and shame. In rich countries, the words "the poor!" provoke the same agitation and panic as the cry "Barbarians!" aroused in the inhabitants of ancient Rome. They anxiously built walls and sent armies to watch their borders. We do the same thing, in different ways, but history tells us it's all pointless.

We cry and protest – and rightly so! – for the children who are prevented from being born, but should we not do as much for the millions of children born and left to die from hunger and sickness, child soldiers forced to engage in war and kill one another for interests to which we in rich countries are not strangers? Could it be that we protest because they belong to our continent and have the same color skin as we do, while the latter belong to another continent and have a different skin color? We protest – and rightly so! – for the elderly, the sick, the malformed who are helped (sometimes encouraged) to die by euthanasia, but should we not do as much for the elderly who die of cold or abandoned to face their fate alone? The laissez-fare law of "live and let live" should never be transformed into the law of "live and let die," as is happening all over the whole world.

The natural law is certainly holy, but precisely to have the strength to observe it we need to start from faith in Jesus Christ. Saint Paul wrote: "For God has done what the law, weakened by the flesh, could not do: he sent his own Son" (*Romans* 8:3). By their moral life, the early Christians helped the State to change its laws; we Christians today cannot do the reverse and think that the State, by its laws, must change people's morals.

3. Love, Help, Evangelize the Poor

The first thing to do, therefore, in relation to the poor, is to break through the double glazing, to overcome our indifference and insensitivity. As the Pope in fact exhorts us, we must become "aware" of the poor, allow ourselves to be gripped by a healthy anxiety over their presence in our midst, often two steps away from our homes. What we are to do for them in practice can be summed up in three words: love them, help them, and evangelize them.

Love the poor. Love for the poor is one of the most common traits of Catholic holiness. In Saint Francis himself, as we saw in the first meditation, love for the poor, starting with the poor Christ, comes before love of poverty, and it was this that led him to espouse poverty. For some Saints, such as Vincent de Paul, Mother Teresa of Calcutta, and countless others, love for the poor was in fact their way to holiness, their charism.

Loving the poor means first of all respecting them and recognizing their dignity. In them, precisely because they lack other incidental titles and secondary distinctions, the radical dignity of being human shines out more brightly than ever. In a Christmas homily given at Milan, Cardinal Montini said: "In the light of Christ, a complete vision of human life sees something more in the poor person than just someone in need. It sees a brother mysteriously invested with a dignity that calls for reverence, a welcoming concern and a compassion beyond what is merely deserved".

However, the poor deserve not only our compassion: they also deserve our admiration. They are humanity's true champions. Every year, cups and medals of gold, silver and bronze are awarded for merit or for winning a race. And all because someone may have managed to run a distance in a shorter time than someone else, or jump a centimetre higher or win a marathon or a slalom competition.

Yet if we could only observe the prowess and endurance the poor are capable of, not just on a single occasion but for a lifetime, the performances of the greatest athletes would seem child's play by comparison. What is a marathon compared to the achievements of a rickshaw man in Calcutta? By the end of his life he has covered the equivalent of several journeys around the world, on foot and in exhausting heat, pulling one or two corpulent passengers along rough roads, over potholes and puddles and darting between cars to avoid being run over.

Francis of Assisi helps us discover an even stronger motive for loving the poor: the fact that they are not simply our "fellow men" or our "neighbors": they are our brothers and sisters! Jesus said: "You have one Father who is in Heaven and you are all brothers" (cf. *Matthew* 23:8-9), but at the time, this word was understood as addressed only to the disciples. In the Christian tradition, a brother in the strict sense is only one who shares the same faith and has received the same Baptism.

Francis takes up Christ's word and gives it a universal significance, which is certainly what Jesus also had in mind. Francis truly "put the whole world in the state of brotherhood."[9] He calls "brothers" not only his friars and companions in the faith, but also lepers, brigands, Saracens, that is, believers and non-believers, the good and bad, above all the poor. He extends the concept of brother and sister - and this is totally new - also to inanimate creatures: the sun, the moon, the earth, water, and finally death. This, evidently, is more a matter of poetry than theology. The Saint knew well that between them and human creatures, made in the image of God, there is the same difference that exists between the son of an artist and the works created by him. But the fact is, the *Poverello's* sense of universal brotherhood is boundless.

[9] D. Vorreux, Saint François d'Assise, Documents, Paris 1968, p. 36.

This issue of brotherhood is the specific contribution that the Christian faith can make to strengthen peace in the world and the struggle against poverty, as the theme of the next World Day of Peace suggests: "Fraternity, Foundation and Path for Peace." If we think about it, this is the only foundation that is real and not utopian. How can it make sense to speak of brotherhood and human solidarity, if one starts from a certain scientific vision of the world which admits "chance and necessity" as the only forces in action in the world? In other words, if one starts from a philosophical vision such as that of Nietzsche, according to whom the world is only the will to power, and any attempt to oppose this is only a sign of the resentment of the weak against the strong"? Those are right who say that "if being is only a matter of chaos and strength, any action that seeks peace and justice is inevitably doomed to remain without foundation."[10] In such a case, there is no sufficient reason to oppose the

_____

[10] V. Mancuso, in La Repubblica, Friday, October 4, 2013.

unbridled laissez-fare of the free market and the "inequity" so forcefully criticized by the Pope in the Exhortation *Evangelii gaudium*.

The duty of loving and respecting the poor is followed by that of *helping* them. Here St James comes to our aid. "What is the point", he asks, "of feeling sorry for a brother or sister without food or clothing, and saying to them: "You poor thing, you're really suffering! Keep warm, and eat plenty", if you don't give them what they need to eat and warm themselves? Like faith, compassion without works is dead". (cf. *Jas* 2:15-17). At the judgment, Christ will not say: "I was naked and you felt sorry for me", but "I was naked and you clothed me" It is not about getting angry with God in face of the misery of the world, but angry with ourselves. One day, a man saw a young girl trembling with cold and crying with hunger. He was seized with a sudden fit of revulsion and cried out: "Oh God, where are you? Why don't you do something for that innocent creature?" But an inner voice replied: "I have done something - I created you!" And he understood at once.

Today, however, mere almsgiving is not enough. The problem of poverty has truly become global. When the Fathers of the Church spoke about the poor they were thinking of the poor of their own city, or at most those of the neighboring city. They hardly knew anything else. In any case, even if they had known, it would have been difficult to provide aid in an economy like theirs. Today we know that almsgiving is not enough, even though nothing can dispense us from doing what we can even on the individual level.

The example of so many men and women of our time shows us that there are so many things that we can do to -- each according to his or her means and possibilities -- to help the poor and to promote their advancement. Speaking of the "cry of the poor" in *Evangelica testificatio*, Paul VI said to us Religious in particular: "It leads some of you to join the poor in their situation and to share their bitter cares. Furthermore, it calls many of your institutes to rededicate for the good of the poor some of their works."[11]

The elimination or reduction of the unjust and scandalous abyss that exists between rich and poor in the world is the most urgent, most enormous task that the recent millennium has handed on to the new century. Let us hope that at the end of this millennium, the same inheritance is not passed on to the next.

Finally, to *evangelize the poor*. This was the mission that Jesus recognized as his own par excellence: "The Spirit of the Lord is upon me, because he has anointed me to preach good news to the poor" (*Luke* 4:18). To the emissaries of the Baptist he pointed to this mission as the sign that the Kingdom was present: "And the poor have good news preached to them" (*Matthew* 11:5). We must not let our guilty conscience lead us to commit the enormous injustice of withholding the good news from those who are its first and

---

[11] Paul VI, *Evangelica testificatio*, 18 (Ench. Vatican 4, p. 651).

most natural recipients, possibly with the excuse that, as the proverb says: "a hungry stomach has no ears".

Jesus multiplied the loaves and the Word together; in fact He first administered the Word, sometimes for three days on end, and then worried about the loaves as well. The poor man does not live on bread alone but also on hope, and on every word that comes from God's mouth. The poor have the inviolable right to hear the Gospel in its entirety, not a reduced, conveniently adapted edition: the Gospel that speaks of love for the poor, but not of hatred for the rich.

4. Joy in Heaven and Joy on Earth

We end on a different note. For Francis of Assisi, Christmas was not only the occasion to weep over Christ's poverty; it was also the feast that had the power to set off all the capacity for joy that was in his heart, and it was immense. At Christmas he literally did foolish things.

> "He wanted the poor and hungry to be
> filled by the rich, and oxen ad asses to be
> spoiled with extra feed and hay. 'If ever I
> speak with the Emperor', he would say, ' I
> will beg him to issue a general decree that
> all who can should throw wheat and grain
> along the roads, so that on the day of such a
> great solemnity the birds may have an
> abundance, especially our sisters the
> larks."[12]

He would become like one of those children whose eyes are full of wonder before the Crib. His biographer tells us that during the Christmas service at Greccio, whenever he spoke the name "Bethlehem" he would fill his mouth with sound and even more with tender affection, producing a sound similar to a bleating sheep. And every time he said "Babe of Bethlehem" or "Jesus," he would lick his lips, as if to relish and retain all the sweetness of those words.[13]

---

[12] Celano, *Vita Secunda*, 151 (ED, II, p. 375).

[13] Celano, Vita Prima, 30 (ED,I,p. 256).

There is a Christmas song that perfectly expresses Saint Francis' sentiments before the Crib, and this comes as no surprise if we remember that its words and music were written, by a Saint like himself, Saint Alphonsus Mary Liguori. Listening to it in the Christmas season, we are moved by its simple but essential message:

From starry skies descending,
Thou comest, glorious King,
A manger low Thy bed,
In winter's icy sting;
O my dearest Child most holy,
Shudd'ring, trembling in the cold!
Thou art the world's Creator,
Yet here no robe, no fire
For Thee, Divine Lord.
Dearest, fairest, sweetest Infant,
Dire this state of poverty.
The more I care for Thee,
Since Thou, o Love Divine,
Will'st now so poor to be.

Index

ZENIT Books

ZENIT Books is an initiative to bring the good news found at ZENIT to you in a new way, expanding our services beyond the e-mail news dispatch, the Web site (zenit.org) and the social networks, all in seven languages. We know our archives contain an inestimable value -- information gathered and stored since ZENIT took its first steps on the net.

We are sure that analyzing, selecting and distributing articles from our archives will be an important service to our readers. With ZENIT Books you will discover works from well-known and new authors.

It is an ambitious and complicated project, but we are convinced that it is necessary to further reflection on topics that have been addressed journalistically, and which continue to merit particular attention.

ZENIT Books is also an alternative source of support for the agency. To acquire a book produced by ZENIT means to support the non-profit international agency independent of ZENIT news – a team of professionals and volunteers.

Our free news service is focused primarily on the Pope's activities: apostolic journeys, documents, meetings with Heads of State and important personalities in the social, cultural and religious realm.

Subscribe for free to ZENIT's daily news service by registering at http://accounts.zenit.org

For information on other publishing initiatives and new publications write to: bookinfo@zenit.org

Made in the USA
Monee, IL
22 December 2019